Egyptian Mythology

Tales from the Egyptian Pantheon

Adam Andino

Table of Contents

Introduction:

A Brief History of Ancient Egypt

"Pharaoh, let my people go!" Moses, a figure in biblical texts, once confronted Pharaoh Ramses to allow his people, the Jews, to leave freely from their enslavement. When the Pharaoh refused, he was met with seven powerful plagues and horrors before finally allowing the Jews to go freely. While this is a powerful story in the Bible speaking about brotherhood and allowing people to be free, it also painted the history of the ancient Egyptian culture as one full of degradation and blasphemy. Due to their polytheistic religious beliefs, Christianity often vilified the ancient Egyptians and their divine right to rule.

Every culture in history had its unique representation of slavery and slave labor. Unfortunately, the enslavement of others is not a new concept but seems to be embedded in human nature. However, the impact of slavery in ancient Egyptian culture was not as prominent as it was portrayed in religious and other texts. While slaves were still used, they were either prisoners of war, offenders of the law, or those who were unable to pay debts. The slaves were not of one certain culture but mainly comprised of those who made the wrong choices in life.

Ancient Egyptian culture was vibrant with life, and they celebrated it so. It was widely known that the ancient Egyptians harbored antagonistic views of other cultures, but they simply stemmed from the belief that their way of life was superior to others. From the kings and Pharaohs to the peasant class, everyone held a role that helped better them as a society.

The Longest-Running Civilization

The Ancient Egyptian civilization lasted over 3000 years, much longer than the infamous Roman Empire by over 1000 years. Their civilization was located on the Nile River in the northern part of Africa, which helped with trade and other economic interests. The land was fertile, so agriculture, and therefore farmers, was a tremendous asset to their civilization. The land was also rich in minerals and building materials such as limestone and granite that helped to further fund their way of life. As a result, three millennia passed with the rise and fall of an empire and numerous dynasties which granted the king (and eventual Pharaoh) the divine right to rule over the civilization.

The Divine Right to Rule

The Pharaohs were granted power simply by being born or married into a dynasty. Following their traditions, the Pharaoh was responsible for the entirety of the civilization. Believed to be hand-picked by the gods, the kings and subsequent Pharaohs, along with other members of their bloodline were granted access to governing the land. As a result, this was the reason behind their lavish lifestyle and riches. Part god, king, and priest, it was the king's responsibility to ensure his people were happy and provided for. This was also known as *ma'at*, or balance and harmony.

In contrast to other civilizations and pantheons, Egyptian culture decreed that written texts were of utmost importance. Scribes, or writers, were tasked with the duties of transcribing and recording all of the day's events, especially of those from higher social classes such as the members of the court and the king. The daily happenings of the upper class were of the utmost significance and interest for the common folk, but some texts about the lives of peasants were also documented.

Daily Living for the Egyptians

Agriculture, one of the most important resources for commerce and trade, impacted the lives of many Egyptians. The lowest class was the peasants and farmers. This did not dissuade their trade, and they thanked the gods for favor in bountiful harvests. However, when the Nile flooded every summer, they were also commissioned to work on the projects of the king and were compensated for it. Some of these projects included building the pyramids.

Smithing and craftsmanship were considered skilled trades. Similar to today's society, those who excelled in their work were also considered for a commission by the kings themselves and other higher-ranking members of society.

The military in the Egyptian kingdom and the later empire was necessary for expanding their borders and making conquests. The Egyptian army was the first organized military system, and they had a record of ensuring their survival. Members of the army were generally conscripted with higher-ranking generals from the upper class and the grunts as peasants and farmers. Typically, if someone was born in a specific class, they remained in that class. In the case of the military, however, they were allowed to move up in the ranks based on both skills in battle and leadership qualities.

Women also had more power than even in some of today's societies. They were allowed to divorce their husbands, own a business, enter contracts with men, and even had the right to abortions. Women could also be priests and have most of the same positions of power the men held such as priesthood, but they could only join the cults of a deity of their same gender. If a woman was married to a peasant, she would not plow the fields but was the homemaker and tasked with rearing children instead. Women typically were not members of the army and often did not desire to be in the military. Both genders wore makeup, more specifically *kohl*, which is essentially close to heavy eyeliner. This use was to save their skin and eyes from the harshness of the sun and reduce glare.

Worshiping the Gods

The Egyptians believed in a polytheistic religion which means they believed in a pantheon of many gods. The gods and goddesses controlled every aspect of life, from agriculture to weather and even death. Most people even went barefoot because the gods did not have footwear, and they wanted to mirror that effect.

One of the most influential effects the deities had on the population was the building of the pyramids themselves. The pyramids were tombs and housed all the king's possessions for his journey into the afterlife. As a result, massive tombs were constructed to ensure their wealth was preserved. In addition, the preservation of bodies was also essential. Mummification and the removal of unnecessary organs including the brain were essential. In the afterlife, kings were then judged by Anubis, the god of death, by weighing the heart for darkness to see if they were worthy of joining the ranks of other kings.

In addition to death, the deities also represented the importance of life and harmony. Temples were erected for each deity, especially those who were more significant. Each deity had specialized rites, rituals, and other ceremonial practices associated with them and their power. Magic was considered to be the base of their power, which, according to the Egyptian creation myth, even predated the gods themselves.

Festivals and entertainment were the pinnacles of peace and harmony reflected in the pantheon and civilization. Most festivals and celebrations were religious-based, which also meant that the people were celebrating through intoxication, giving thanks to that deity, and asking for a favor in the future. One example of a lavish festival was the Bast Festival, which celebrated the birth of Bastet, goddess of fertility, cats, and women. The festival only lasted for a day, but it was one of the most popular. Some texts claimed that as many as 700,000 people attended the festival at its peak. It was a day full of dancing, drinking, and music.

The gods and goddesses were an essential part of everyday life for the ancient Egyptians. Priests would feed the statues of the gods they served three times a day. Prayers and rituals were performed daily by all members of society. All forms of writing were considered a record of time with deities reigning over their eternal libraries. The gods reigned supreme over every aspect of life and even death. The next chapter will go over a list of the main deities and what they reigned over.

Chapter 1: 14 Main Gods and Goddesses

The ancient Egyptian pantheon inspires awe and creativity still today. Countless artists have been inspired by the Egyptians, and films such as *The Mummy* have created a renaissance of interest in Egyptian mythology. Due to the amount of mythological lore and historical records, the Egyptian pantheon is one of the most complete in the realm of mythology. Fourteen of the main gods and goddesses are listed and described further below. Some of these deities have several name spellings, which are also included.

Amun (Amon): God of Air

Amun, known as Amun-Ra in the later years of mythology, was the god of air. Originally, Amun was a minor fertility god and a patron deity of Thebes, but in later creation myths of the civilization, he was one of the creators of the world. His name was believed to mean 'the Hidden One,' but there is still an air of mystery to his etymology. Amun was usually depicted wearing a crown that was massive in height and split into two.

After the battle in Hyksos when the Egyptians emerged victorious, Amun became one of the most important gods in the pantheon. He was fused with Ra towards the end of the civilization, resulting in the two deities becoming the most powerful beings within the mythology.

Anubis: God of Death and Embalming

Anubis is perhaps one of the most famous of all the deities. Portrayed as a man with a jackal's head, he was the god of death, more specifically the god of embalming and funeral care, and he was most notable for his role in the ritual each soul undergoes after death. It was believed that he not only escorted the dead through the Hall of Truth before the ritual, but he was also the one who performed the ritual. In the 'Weighing of the Heart,' the heart of the deceased would be weighed against the feather of Ma'at, the goddess of justice. If the heart was as heavy as or lighter than the feather, they were granted access to the paradise of the afterlife. However, if it was heavier due to the numerous injustices in their heart, then their soul would be fed to Ammit or the soul-devourer.

Anubis and his family were rife with betrayal. His father was Osiris, the god of the dead, and his mother was Nephthys, the goddess of funerals. After Set, who was both the husband and brother of Nephthys, abandoned her, Anubis went to live with Osiris and his wife Isis. The completion of this myth will be covered in Chapter 4.

Bastet (Bast): Goddess of Cats and the Hearth

Bastet, as mentioned in the title, was the goddess of the hearth, fertility, childbirth, and of course, cats. She was the daughter of the sun god Ra and was often connected to Horus. She warded off evil in the home and for the women and children inside it. In the early part of the civilization, she was a goddess who was depicted as a woman with a lion's head; as the years progressed, her depiction switched to a regal-looking cat with rings in her nose.

She was extremely popular among the Egyptians, and she was known for granting favors to those who asked during her festival. She was a favorite of the women, especially during the festival in her name. In addition, she was the reason cats were considered sacred within the civilization. Cats were not to be harmed for any reason, for it was believed that any cat was her incarnate.

Hathor: Goddess of Love and Joy

Hathor was another daughter of Ra and, therefore, sister to Bastet. She was also the wife of Horus. She was often depicted with horns on her head, or like cattle, and was a powerful goddess. She was the goddess of joy, love, beauty, celebration, women, childbirth, and even drunkenness. One of her positions was to guide souls into the afterlife, and she also defended the sun barge of Ra from Apep, a myth that will be covered in Chapter 3.

Heka: God of Medicine and Healing

Heka was one of the oldest but most important gods in the Egyptian pantheon. He was the god of medicine and healing, which was a crucial part of the culture. Physicians and doctors worshiped this deity, not only due to his powers of healing, but his command over magic as well. Since magic was imbued in all aspects of Egyptian culture, this deity was also considered to be the source of all power in the universe.

He was one of the first gods to exist, predating even Ra. In later myths, however, he was considered to be the son of Khnum and Menhet. Often, he was depicted with a staff equipped at all times, and later myths told the tale of how his staff was then interwoven with two serpents.

Horus: God of Kingship

Horus had a unique story in his development as a god. In the early years of ancient Egyptian mythology, he was seen as one of the five gods in the creation myth, presiding over the sun, power, and sky. He was portrayed either as a hawk or a man with the head of a hawk. At this stage, he was known as Horus the Elder and was considered to be one of the most important deities, alongside his four siblings Osiris, Iris, Set, and Nephthys.

His later version, Horus the Younger, was the more popular of the two. As the myths of Horus the Younger became more prominent, so too did his popularity. In this myth, Horus was the son of Osiris and Isis. He was also associated with divine rule, and it was believed that all the kings and pharaohs were Horus incarnate. This explained the many dynasties of the civilization, and therefore, each king channeled the god during life. The myth of Horus and his ascension to the throne will be more detailed in Chapter 4.

Isis: Goddess of Secrets and Magic

Isis, the goddess of essentially every aspect of Egyptian civilization, was known as the 'Mother of the Gods.' She was the wife and sister of Osiris, and they had Horus the Younger together. Her other siblings included Set, Nephthys, and Horus the Elder. She often cared for people during their life and guided them to the afterlife. She was the goddess of secrets and magic and therefore was one of the most powerful deities in the pantheon. Her myths, especially the one revolving around the death of her husband Osiris, were considered to be some of the most important stories to the ancient Egyptians.

In a depiction of Isis and Horus the Younger, she is seen cradling her son. Similarly, Christian iconography portrays the Virgin Mary cradling her son Jesus. Because she cared for people in every stage of life, she was a crucial part of the Egyptian pantheon and was worshiped by all. Isis was one of the longest-reigning deities in any pantheon, ranging from the earliest Egyptian civilizations and expanding into both Greece and Rome. During the Roman Empire and its fall, there was a cult specifically dedicated to Isis. This cult was one of the main sources of resistance to the new Christian faith. As a result, her likeness influenced the Christian religion through images of Mary and Jesus.

Ma'at: Goddess of Harmony

Ma'at was at the heart of the culture of ancient Egypt. Her name translates to 'harmony'—one of the core building blocks of civilization. She was the goddess of justice, truth, and of course, harmony. She was also the one who controlled the changing of the seasons and positioned the stars in the sky at night. Often portrayed as a woman wearing a diadem with an ostrich feather, she accompanied all in their walks of life and was present when their souls were judged. She was a revered goddess throughout the pantheon.

Osiris: God of the Underworld

Osiris, another most famous deity, was the brother of Isis, Set, Horus the Elder, and Nephthys. His wife was his sister Isis, and he had two sons: Horus the Younger and an adopted son Anubis. As the god of death and the Underworld, he was tasked with overseeing the Underworld alongside Anubis. In early mythology, he was a god of fertility and later became the first ruler over the people of Egypt. He was often depicted as a mummy with greenish-black skin, complete with embalming. This not only symbolized his involvement with the dead but it also illustrated his influence over the Nile, and therefore, fertility.

The Book of the Dead, one of the most famous books from the ancient Egyptian era, portrayed him as one of the judges in the Weighing of the Heart ritual after death. He was one of the first deities to represent resurrection and was believed to influence the Roman Empire's cult of Isis. The myth revolving around his death will be explored in greater detail in Chapter 6.

Ptah: God of Truth

Ptah was considered to be the original god before the rest in ancient Egyptian mythology. The creation of the universe and the first gods themselves was a part of his design. He was the god of truth and the patron deity of the city of Memphis around 3000 BCE. In addition, he reigned over artisans and craftsmanship. This extended to those who were architects, designing and constructing buildings. He was often depicted as a mummy wearing a headpiece.

Ra (Amun-Ra, Re, Atum): God of the Sun

Ra, in addition to other gods, was responsible for the creation of the earth and its people. He was the god of the sun and supreme creator, who had several myths to his name, including the creation myth. He was responsible for the day turning into night and vice versa, which resulted in a myth about one of his arch-enemies, Apep, the serpent who battled with him over the domination of the world. Ra was depicted as a hawk or a man with the head of a hawk.

According to different texts and translations of the creation myth, Ra and Amun were often used in place of each other. In some texts, Ra was the supreme creator of the universe and the land, while others claimed he simply played a part in the creation. Ra was believed to be the father of Tefnut and Shu, the deities of heat and air respectively, but only according to some versions of the myth.

Seshat: Goddess of Writing and Measurements

Seshat was the goddess of writing, measurements, books, and records. She was deemed the patroness of both private and public libraries and welcomed all to experience literacy. Her husband Thoth was the god of writing as well as wisdom. However, her expertise in measurements made her memorable. Often, the king would pay tribute to this goddess to ensure he made the precise measurements for each building constructed. As a result, builders and architects paid tribute to her as well. While she did not have a designated temple of her own, she was an important deity to scribes as well. Seshat was depicted with a leopard skin on top of her robe and equipped with a writing tablet in her right hand, representing her love for the written word.

Set (Seth): God of Chaos

Set, or Seth, was the infamous god of chaos, deserts, storms, and war. He was married to his sister Nephthys and was the brother of Osiris, Horus the Elder, and Isis. However, he is currently best known as the first murderer in written text. Set was seen as the necessary evil to create balance and be an antagonist to the benevolent gods Horus and Osiris. Often he was portrayed to have the hooves of a bull and the crimson body of a beast with a forked tail, similar to what the Christians painted their Satan character as.

Set was a troubled god, filled with rage and jealousy which boiled over into the killing of his brother. However, he did have a redemption arc. As part of his recompense, he aided Ra in the nightly battle against the serpent Apep for domination over the skies.

Thoth: God of Writing and Wisdom

Thoth was the god of writing and wisdom, alongside his wife Seshat. He was the deity who created spoken language and the inventor of hieroglyphic writing. Similar to his wife, he was one of the gods who scribes most often worshiped. In some texts, it was determined he was a minor sun god alongside his father Ra, but others claimed that he was the son of Horus the Younger. He was always on the side of humans, even to the point of giving them the gift of language and writing. He was portrayed as a baboon in some texts, but most of the time he was portrayed as a man with the head of an ibis, a bird similar to the pelican but of subtropical climates.

In addition to writing, Thoth was the god of wisdom and had access to secrets and magic that the other gods did not. As a result, he was considered one of the wisest deities in the pantheon. He was responsible for conducting the weighing of the hearts, then reported his findings to Anubis and Osiris, who then judged the soul.

While there are over a hundred individual deities representing a certain part of human life, there are many that overlap in different areas. As a whole, each god or goddess had unique perspectives and personalities, different animal attributes and aesthetics, and even their own tastes in clothing and self-presentation. With over 3000 years of changing mythologies, there is a rich lore associated with this pantheon. In the next chapter, there will be more information on the creatures, monsters, and demigods of this ancient mythology.

Chapter 2: Creatures, Monsters, and Demigods

The creatures, monsters, and demigods of the Egyptian pantheon are few. Each of the characters represented in this chapter was an important figure who was often tasked with guarding a certain place or even as a representation of an animal. Many of the creatures were chimeras; therefore, they inspired both awe and fear in those who listened to stories or read about them. Each creature, monster, or demigod was imbued with some sort of magical power which they used in defense or to create chaos.

Creatures and Monsters

As with any mythology, there is always a section dedicated to the many myths and legends of the creatures within it. The Egyptian pantheon is no different. Due to the anthropomorphic nature of the deities themselves, it can be difficult to differentiate between a deity and a monster. Some of the creatures listed below can even be classified as deities based on their powers, but their appearances and stories were created to persuade children into behaving, and as such, they are included here. Below are some of the creatures from Egyptian mythology listed alphabetically.

Ammit (Ammut)

Ammit was one of the goddesses of the Underworld, but she reigned supreme in judging the goodness of the souls of the dead. She was a chimera with the head of a crocodile, the body of a lion, and the back end of a hippopotamus. Also known as 'the devourer of souls,' she was most notable for her role when a soul was filled with sin. Not only did she represent the manifestation of all predatory animals to the Egyptian people, but she also represented the fear of a second death. If a soul was deemed unworthy, Ammit devoured it, sending it to a flaming purgatory.

Apep (Apophis)

Apep held one of the leading roles in the myth of Ra and the setting sun. He was the serpent who tried to murder Ra every morning before the sun rose in the sky. Ra and several other deities went through the Underworld before making their way to the horizon for sunrise where Apep waited for the disastrous encounter. Considered the complete opposite of the gods who reveled in order, Apep embodied darkness and chaos. Some legends stated that earthquakes were caused by Apep moving under the earth and that violent desert storms were because of Apep and Set engaging in battle.

It was believed that the serpent existed in the universe before the arrival of gods, and he wanted it to return to the same state as before the existence of life. However, some texts were written that Apep was born after Ra and came from his umbilical cord.

This representation of the origin of Apep was symbolic of the constant war between light and dark, order and chaos.

The Griffin

The origins of the Griffin were often wrapped in mystery. No one truly knows of their origin myth in Egyptian mythology, but their essence was transposed into other mythologies and legends. The creature was a chimera with the head, wings, and talons of an eagle but with the muscular body of a lion. The Griffin was fierce-looking and was thought to be a symbol of war and bravery. However, it also had two other attributes as well: one as the guardian of treasures and secrets, the other as a defender against evil magic.

There has been one depiction of the Griffin found that dates back to around 3100 BCE. It was found on a palette, which was later named 'Two Dog Palette.' On its surface, there was the depiction of the Griffin as well as the Serpopard, which will be discussed next.

The Serpopard

The Serpopard was another chimera, combining attributes of a leopard and a serpent. In its few depictions, it was showcased as a creature with the body of a leopard, the long neck of a serpent, and the head of either a serpent or a leopard. Interestingly, there is some speculation that the head could be a lion instead of a leopard, but this remains another mystery.

Just like the Griffin, there is no known origin story of the Serpopard, but there were many inscriptions of it on vases and other forms of decoration. It was believed to be the symbolic representation of the chaos outside the borders of the kingdom. Many of these depictions were of these mythical beings being killed as a way to conquer the fears of the chaos beyond the kingdom. However, there were also instances of two Serpopards with their necks intertwined, which also represented vitality and cooperation.

Sphynx

The last creature on this list is perhaps the most famous. The Sphynx was immortalized in the Egyptian kingdom by the construction of its likeness in Giza next to the three pyramids made exclusively for Ra. However, it was also a prominent feature located in the palaces and temples, as it was painted in murals and even had statues dedicated to the creature.

The Sphynx was another chimera but constructed of both human and animal elements. It had the head of a human, which closely mirrored the appearances of pharaohs and kings, grafted with the body of a lion. However, this beast was also associated with Ra, as they also had the heads of falcons and rams. The head of a human—more specifically, a king or Pharaoh—represented the power the king possessed.

The Sphynx was also the protector of tombs, which explains its positioning near the three tombs in Giza. It is most known for asking for the answers to three riddles as part of a trial to enter the tomb and the many treasures and secrets that came along with it.

Demigods

The film *The Mummy* inspired a new generation of archaeologists who were eager to learn more about ancient Egyptian culture. While completely fictional, it did take some source material seriously and incorporated it into the action-adventure film. Imhotep was a real demigod in ancient Egyptian myth, but not in the way he was portrayed in the film. In this section, we discuss two demigods of note who are either minor deities or were deified after death.

Apis

Apis was a bull who was believed to be the son of Ptah. Not much is known about this particular demigod. Mainly, however, he was the sacred bull of Memphis and was worshiped as such. He was not a demigod in the traditional sense, but he was still a figure who was worshiped as a sacred being. Originally with a black coat, Apis was symbolic of those with strong hearts, but he was also a herald of Ptah as well.

Imhotep

Imhotep, thanks to modern-day film, was portrayed as a civil officer of king Djoser around 2600 BCE before he ascended into godhood. In life, he was responsible for the design and construction of the Step Pyramid built in his lifetime. It was a great accomplishment, so much so that he was considered to be one of the most famous architects in ancient Egypt.

Not only were his architectural skills in demand but so were his wisdom and intellect. Imhotep was the author of many texts about wisdom, medicine, and even mathematics. Whether or not Imhotep was a real historical figure is a mystery due to the lack of information on his life, but after his death, he was deified. In the process of history evolving into myth and legend, it was believed that Imhotep was the son of Thoth, the god of architecture.

The mix of creatures and deities often was a fine line to cross. While many of the creatures, monsters, and demigods were, in some way, a deity themselves, often they were seen as guardians or symbols. These symbols are often transformed into the main themes and morals that are embedded within the myths themselves. But how did this all begin? The answer will be revealed in the next chapter where we discuss the creation myths of the Egyptian pantheon.

Chapter 3: The Creation Myths

One of the most intriguing aspects of the Egyptian creation myth is that it contains several variations of the same myth. This is to be expected, as varying translations and contexts can be difficult to determine. Within this chapter, there are three parts to the creation myth, each representing a city with its respective main deity. These cities were Hermopolis, Memphis, and Heliopolis with the gods Amun, Ptah, and Ra, respectively. It can be said that each myth can either build upon the other or they can take place at the same time. However, each myth was—and still is—open to interpretation.

Creation Myth 1: Amun

The first creation myth concerns itself with the presence of Amun. In Hermopolis, known to the Egyptians as Khemnu instead of its Greek name, Amun was their version of Ra, the reigning supreme god and creator of the universe. In this version of the myth, the world was engulfed in water. There originally was no sign of life anywhere to be found for thousands of years. It was in this same water, however, that the first creation of gods commenced.

The Ogdoad

As the waters swirled for many years, the vast ocean eventually birthed eight supernatural beings who would later become gods. Four males and four females were born out of the chaotic destruction of the waves. Each male and female were matched in pairs with similar names and attributes. The deities that arose from the depths were known as Kek and Kauket, the deities of darkness and ambiguity; Heh and Heuhet the deities of timelessness; Nun and Naunet, the deities of the early cosmic disorder resulting in their birth; and Amun and Amaunet, the deities of the air and sun.

Unfortunately, there are few details further illustrating the myth written in narrative form. It was believed by the Egyptians that the rest of creation transpired in a mystical egg belonging to either an ibis or goose, signifying the birth of the creator of all gods. It was then that the sun god Amun arose in power and laid the foundation for the myths to follow. The rest was open to interpretation from the reason for the gods' existence to even their appearance.

The original inhabitants of Hermopolis believed that this narrative of the myth would symbolize the mystery and intrigue of the beginnings of the gods and even be representative of the gods themselves. Because this myth was shrouded in so much mystery, it exemplified the gods and their mysticism. However, it is believed that these deities were not only the oldest of the gods but, instead, were also responsible for the creation of the gods in the Ennead which were the next generation of gods.

Creation Myth 2: Ptah

Ptah's story started in Memphis which was the prime center of government in the empire for many millennia. During this time, the god Ptah emerged and became the supreme deity according to the lore in Memphis. In this myth, the gods are portrayed in their human forms as the result of their birth.

According to this myth, Ptah was the first being to come into existence. At first, his existence was synonymous with the first patch of dry land in the vastness of the ocean. Once he emerged into his human form, he appeared to be quite handsome. He was often portrayed as a mummy with one arm free to hold his staff. He also had a shaved head and wore a skull cap.

Ptah, in addition to being incredibly handsome, was also known for his architectural brilliance. He looked at his surroundings and, seeing them bare, wanted to make a more habitable location for himself. He imagined the world he wanted, then spoke it into existence with his heart. This encompassed all landscapes and life, including humans.

However, this was a process. One of his first creations as a god was to make more beings like him. In one breath, he spoke into existence Atum, Shu, Nephthys, Osiris, Iris, Tefnut, Nut, and Set. These deities represented both natural and political order and were thought to be the most important to Ptah.

After he created the gods, Ptah then built the foundation of Egypt, both in the physical landscape as well as the people within it. He created man and the wildlife which surrounded Egypt. He then tasked the other gods and goddesses with watching over humanity, but he was the overseer of all.

Creation Myth 3: Ra

This creation myth is perhaps the most complete of the three. The myth surrounding Ra (Atum) is more rounded and includes much more detail than the previous two. Due to ancient writings such as the *Pyramid Texts*, there is more reference material so, therefore, more details of this myth are known. Heliopolis, at this time in history, was the epicenter for the beginning of the pharaohs. As a result, this myth became one of the more dominant creation myths in the pantheon. In the myth, Ra was named Atum, so for clarity, Ra will be referred to as Atum to keep the initial root of the mythology.

The Ennead

Not to be confused with Virgil's *Aeneid*, the epic poem chronicling the life of Aeneas, the Ennead was the combination of the eight deities that were created after the existence of Atum. Similar to the previous creation myth of Hermopolis, these deities were male and female counterparts in pairs. However, the figures in this myth are different from the Hermopolis creation myth.

In the beginning, the world was shrouded in darkness. This darkness was known as the Void, where nothing—including light—existed. The Void was nothing but dark water and swirled with chaotic storms. The god of magic, Heka, waited for the correct moment for creation to begin. When all was still, the god of water Nu allowed a mound to arise from the watery depths of the ocean. This mound was also known as the *ben-ben*, which would then become Heliopolis.

From this mound, a figure appeared out of a pillar on top of the ben-ben. He was in his mortal form and was considered by the Egyptians to be extremely handsome. He gazed around him at the infinite nothingness, realizing that he was alone. The creation of the next deities, Shu, the god of air, and Tefnut, the goddess of moisture, came next. In some versions of the myth, he had relations with his shadow and then birthed the deities. Others claim that Atum masturbated on the mound where the pillar stood and that the god and goddess were born that way. Another version claimed that the deities were created by his spit and vomit.

The Birth of the Gods

After these gods were birthed, they were tasked with building the foundation of order and life itself on the earth. The pair left their father on the ben-ben and created the foundation of all life and order. However, their father was upset because he was, yet again, alone. He sent out his left eye, later known as the Eye of Ra, and searched for them. When his children came back to see their father and to return his eye, Atum wept because he was so pleased to see them. The resulting tears fell onto the mound and birthed the first man and woman.

Because these new creatures had nowhere to live, Tefnut and Shu copulated and birthed twins: the god of the earth, Geb, and goddess of the sky, Nut. The pair created a home for the new beings, so they could further their growth. Geb and Nut, however, fell deeply in love with one another despite being siblings. The pair never separated and were always close to one another. This incestuous nonsense, according to Atum, needed to stop permanently. As a result, he separated Geb and Nut for all eternity. He sent Nut above in the heavens while Geb remained steadfast on Earth, and the two were never allowed to touch again.

Some of the portrayals of Geb and Nut were provocative, with many of the depictions sexual in nature. One depiction of this union within the *Book of the Dead* was of Geb nude in his human form aligning himself with Nut, who was also naked but with stars on her figure. In that same portrayal, Atum began to separate the pair.

However, Nut was already pregnant with her children. As she remained in the sky, she gave birth to her children Osiris, Iris, Horus the Elder, Nephthys, and Set. As the children grew, so did their attributes and personalities. Osiris, being the firstborn of the five, proved himself to be intellectual with judicial authority. Set was the harbinger of chaos and was deeply jealous of his brother. Isis was the most selfless of the five, earning her place at the side of Osiris as his wife. Her sister Nephthys was a foil of Isis's character—the balance of darkness to her light. Nephthys paired well with Set, as Set was also quite the opposite of Osiris. Horace the Elder, the god of air, essentially became the next Atum.

The Beginnings of a Rivalry

As the human population grew, so did the need for order and harmony. As a result, Atum appointed Osiris and Isis as the deities to rule over the land. Atum had other situations he needed to attend to and left his great-grandson to his devices. Osiris ruled for many years as the main god of the Egyptians, creating a long period where all was peaceful and in order. However, this was not to last because of the intense jealousy Set had toward his brother. This myth revolving around Set and Osiris will be covered more fully in the next chapter, along with its many twists along the way.

Conclusion

This chapter included the three myths relating to the creation of the world and Egypt. The Egyptian pantheon differed between locations due to there being separate creation myths. Because there were three distinct cities with their own patron god starring in the myth, the myths include distinct variations from each other. While some may argue that the myth revolving around Ra (Atum) was the most important, the many facets and variations only add to its richness. In the next chapter, the exciting myth of Osiris and Set will be revealed, full of betrayal, adultery, and murder.

Chapter 4: The First Recorded Fratricide

The first recording of fratricide and murder was the inspiration for many stories in various mythologies around the world. As mentioned in the previous chapter, Set's jealousy toward his brother boiled over in a climactic and exciting tale. This myth revolved around the many betrayals of Set and his sister-wife Nephthys toward Osiris and Isis. With their deception, it brought about a time of upheaval and chaos within the ancient world.

The Burden of Jealousy

Osiris and Set were two of the five siblings of the goddess Nut. Osiris, proving he was the best ruler of the five, was appointed the supreme god of Heliopolis. For many years, all was peaceful in the realm of man and god. Osiris instructed the men about plowing fields, keeping domesticated animals such as cattle, and planting the correct plants at the correct time, in addition to creating law and order among them. Osiris was seen as the first true pharaoh of the kingdom, ensuring that everyone was doing their part in society.

It was believed that his wife, Isis, then taught the women how to use the crops their husbands planted to cook meals, as well as how to weave fabric into clothing for protection from the elements and for fashion. She also taught the women how to raise children and protected them from harm. Her magical abilities ensured that both men and women were created equal in a partnership through marriage.

Set and Nephthys

Set was immensely jealous of his brother's reign and powers. As the years progressed, the more his anger and jealousy festered. He considered himself to be passed over for the chance at being a leader, and he even had a vision of his own for society.

Nephthys, in a similar way, was immensely jealous of her sister as well. She was not only jealous of the power of life that Isis possessed, but she was also jealous that Isis was married to her attractive brother. Tired of her role as only the funerary goddess, Nephthys hatched a plan of lustful vengeance over her sister.

The First Affair

Nephthys had an immense lustful passion for her brother Osiris. One day when he was alone, Nephthys concealed her true identity and donned the appearance of Isis. With seduction on her mind, it was easy to fool Osiris into believing that the true Isis was the one instigating the love-making. The two had an affair unbeknownst to Osiris, and Nephthys quickly fell pregnant with her son Anubis. She had not predicted this would happen and only wanted the smug satisfaction of her vengeance to be successful.

Nephthys hid the pregnancy from Set and the rest of their family. She feared the wrath of Set and knew that if he ever found out, it would cause an untold amount of havoc for both Anubis and Osiris. When Anubis was born, Set discovered her betrayal and abandoned her and the child. She gave the child to Osiris and Isis, fearing for her safety and the safety of her child.

The Plotting of Revenge

Set had always been jealous of his brother for his supreme power and love of the people, but compounded with the knowledge of his wife's affair, the scales tipped closer to unbridled chaos. The god was deeply angered and hurt over his wife's betrayal of the sanctity of their marriage, so much so that he abandoned Nephthys to pursue his plot for revenge.

As each year passed, Set plotted the death of his brother. He knew it needed to be soon, and each passing moment filled him with more rage. In this preparation for revenge, he secretly received his brother's exact measurements for an ornate chest to be made with the best craftsmanship. As the chest was constructed, he plotted a way to make his brother enter the chest of his own accord.

As the chest neared completion, Set plotted out every minute detail for his plan to work. He decided to throw a great feast to which Osiris and others were invited.

Time for a Feast

With all the careful plotting in motion, Set was able to create a game to provoke his brother's murder. The chest was to be the main focal point after the feast was finished. After everyone was present, the feast began. Sounds of laughter rang along the walls, and the smell of food was intoxicating. Everyone seemed to be having a great time, and Set started to imply that he had organized a game with a grand prize at the end.

Once the feast was finished, Set announced that the game was to begin. He led everyone to the location of the beautifully ornate chest, where all stood in awe. Set presented them with the game: to see if anyone could figure out for whom this chest was designed. He then gave them the hint that to truly figure it out, everyone had to climb in and see if it fit them.

The gods and goddesses all wanted this beautiful chest, so they eagerly took turns trying to climb into the chest. No one fit in it. Osiris, curious to see if it would fit him, was the last to climb inside of it. Shocked, he proudly proclaimed that the chest fit him, and therefore he was now the proud owner of it.

In a rush, Set slammed down the lid on top of Osiris, trapping him inside. Set told the audience that he would return Osiris to his home, so he could fully appreciate the material inside. However, this was not the case.

Instead of returning the god of kingship to his home, Set instead threw Osiris into the Nile where he drowned. When he returned to Heliopolis, Set announced that Osiris was dead and pronounced himself as ruler. With the god of chaos as king, the world fell into disrepair and darkness. Isis and the rest of the Egyptians grieved the loss of their king.

The Dismemberment

When Set returned from the murder of Osiris, Isis was suspicious of her husband's death. In haste, she searched for her husband with the help of the people. As they hunted for her husband, they trudged through the flooded waters of the Nile. Eventually, they found the infamous chest inside a tree near a city called Byblos. When she and those who helped her discovered the chest, they removed it from the tree to find the body of Osiris inside. In gratitude for the people's help, Isis granted them the ability to make papyrus, an invention to help people write down important documents. This detail, however, may have later been added to further solidify the Egyptians' main export of papyrus.

Hiding the Body from an Enraged God

Isis carried the body back to Heliopolis to resurrect him from the dead. She hid the body in a safe place and tasked her sister Nephthys to guard the body. In the meantime, she gathered the necessary spells, potions, and ingredients to ensure a full resurrection. Nephthys readily agreed to guard the body of Osiris; her guilt over the previous affair with him had festered, and she wanted to make it up to her sister.

Set, at this point, grew suspicious of Isis and was deeply concerned that she would find the body of his brother and attempt to resurrect him. He looked for her but discovered that she had left. He was well aware of Isis's magical ability, intelligence, and resourcefulness, so he decided to corner his wife and ask if she had discovered the body.

With great defiance, Nephthys lied and told him that no, Isis had not discovered the body. However, Set knew when his wife was deceiving him. He further interrogated her until she finally revealed the location of the body and what Isis had planned for it.

The Unspeakable Horror

After forcing his wife to tell him the location of the body, Set jumped into action. He arranged for his henchmen to retrieve the body from its hiding spot. A short time passed, and the henchmen returned with the body. He shooed his men away and resorted to the only logical way of dispensing the body to ensure the resurrection wouldn't happen. He needed to dismember it.

He laid the deceased body on a table in front of him, where he proceeded to cut his brother into pieces. In some versions of this myth, the number of pieces was 14, while other versions claimed 42. To further emphasize the horrific crime, this book will reference the latter.

After the body was fully dismembered, Set raced to the Nile and dispersed the remains. In his mind, if even one piece was missing, the resurrection was doomed. Proud of his achievement and confident that Isis would never find all the pieces, Set returned to his home.

Resurrection

Meanwhile, Isis returned to the secret location after gathering all the necessary equipment to bring Osiris back from the dead. When she arrived at the location, she gazed at the sight in front of her. The chest had been broken into and the body of her husband was missing. She knew Set was behind this disappearance, and she fell to her knees in grief and rage. Tears silently slid down her cheeks as she wept.

Nephthys had arrived to find her sister weeping on the ground. She felt ashamed and guilty for giving away the location of the body. Knowing what Set had done, she informed Isis. She started with an apology for ruining her sister's chance to be reunited with her husband, then suggested they look for the remains together.

Isis agreed to the arrangement, eager to find each of the 42 parts. As each piece floated by them along the Nile, they buried it under a mound with a guardian to protect it from Set and his minions. It was believed that each part buried under their mounds was a representation of the eventual 42 provinces of Egypt; the lore being that the two goddesses had founded these provinces.

Once most of the pieces had been gathered, the two goddesses rebuilt the body of Osiris. More pieces were gathered until all but one had been found: the penis, which was supposedly eaten by a fish in the river. However, the goddesses were not dissuaded. Isis manufactured a replacement for the penis and placed it on his body. Anubis, who had grown into adulthood, helped bring his father back to life by embalming him, further mummifying him. In addition to his mother's incantations, potions, and herbs, Anubis and Isis revived him, but only for a few moments. In that brief window of time, Horace the Younger was conceived.

Because of his incompleteness, Osiris could no longer rule over the land. Instead, he was tasked with going to the Underworld and using his newfound power over death to judge and reign over the souls of the deceased.

The Birth of Horus the Younger

Isis was forced to hide her pregnancy from Set for fear that Set would also have her and her child killed. When it came time for her to give birth, she cast protective spells over him, so Set would never discover the child. She named the child Horus, a child who was destined to bring peace and harmony back to the land of Egypt. The people, as well as the deities themselves, longed for the day when Horus would challenge his uncle and reclaim the throne. Unfortunately, the time for Horace to reclaim the throne was a long wait for the kingdom.

Conclusion

This myth was the first of its kind with its many shocking and disturbing scenarios. From fratricide to dismemberment, adultery, and even necrophilia, this myth encompassed a fair number of taboos and inexplicable horrors. Not only did this myth serve to further explain the relationship and dynamics of the gods, but it also served as a cautionary tale. It warned the audience of the dangers of intense jealousy and the chaos jealousy could bring. In the next chapter, the downfall of Set because of Horus the Younger will further illustrate the product of this jealousy.

Chapter 5: The Battle Between

Set and Horus

The final installment of this myth constitutes the personification of the battle between good and evil, order and chaos. The rivalry between Set and Horus was considered to be the most intense and bitter conflict in all of Egyptian mythology. The deities fought among each other for 80 years before one claimed the throne for himself. In the meantime, before Horus grew into adulthood, Set had sent his minions to discover the whereabouts of both Isis and the new child.

The Childhood of Horus

Through the many years of waiting for Horus to become fully realized, the kingdom fell into even more disarray. Darkness and despair overtook the land, and the people struggled to survive. Nowhere was safe, and the people had to endure the lifestyle wrought upon by Set, including the pregnant goddess and her unborn child. Set soon learned of the pregnancy and recruited his henchmen to find Isis.

Hiding in Plain Sight

Once Isis realized that Set's henchmen were tasked with tracking her down and killing her and the baby, she immediately went into hiding. She was aided by her sister and the god Thoth in the casting of protection spells to prevent Set from finding her. Isis was renowned for her magical abilities and mastery of potions and used her skills to ward off potential threats. She hid and gave birth in a swampy section of the Nile where few ventured, allowing her to raise her son in peace. She named her son Horus to honor her brother and as a beacon of hope for the people of Egypt.

As the child matured into adulthood, he and his mother were still forced to hide in the bowels of the swamp. Horus grew up listening to his mother recounting tales of his late father. As he became older, she explained the depths of his uncle's deception. During that time, Isis and Horus kept watching over each other, grateful for the incantations that aided their secrecy. Set's henchmen searched for them to no avail and would always return to Set empty-handed.

Set knew the pair was still out there, biding their time for Horus to grow into maturity. He knew that this was a recipe for his permanent demise, so he continued to search for them. He was never discouraged, and his anger inspired fear in the hearts of his henchmen, who still searched for evidence of their survival.

Horus's childhood was rife with danger. Even though he knew of his mother's powerful incantations, there was always a fear of discovery. Danger lurked behind every part of the swamp. Unfortunately, there are no known stories of the childhood of Horus and how he navigated through the many dangers of the swamp and Set's henchmen.

Horus and Set Finally Meet

Once Horus became of age, Isis released the spells of protection around the pair. He had grown into a handsome man with battle and intellectual skills to match. However, he was not after love but vengeance, instead. He made his way to the throne where he challenged his uncle to many duels.

The story of Horus's journey to the throne is not fully known in detail, but it appeared that Set was waiting for him to reveal himself after many years in hiding. Set discarded the extra guards around his kingdom and patiently awaited Horus's arrival at the throne.

Set did not need to wait long. He gazed upon his future rival as he entered the throne room and demanded his birthright. Set, however, was amused that such a young god would dare to challenge him, but he agreed to the challenge, nonetheless.

The Battle for Dominance

Over 80 years, the two gods engaged in petty, bitter rivalries and contests over who was the most deserving of the throne. At first, the dispute was to be settled by sparring in a duel. Set was confident in his abilities to overcome his contender due to his many years of existence. Horus's capabilities paled in comparison due to a lack of experience. This was a duel that Set knew he could win.

What Set did not know was that Horus had spent his time in hiding training for this very moment. Additionally, Horus was enraged at the poor treatment of his father, his mother, and all the people of Egypt. He longed for justice and peace to be restored to the kingdom under his rule.

The two engaged in a duel, but the pair of them were evenly matched in strength. Each tried to overthrow the other, but it was futile on both ends. They engaged in numerous duels, trying to overtake the other, but each duel ended in a draw. They could not best one another, so they approached a trifecta of gods for trials to settle the dispute once and for all.

The Trials for the Throne

After Set and Horus called together a tribunal of the most powerful deities in the realm, the three gods emerged and listened to both sides. Each claimed that the throne was theirs, and the three gods Ra, Shu, and Thoth, the gods of the sun, air, and wisdom respectively, listened with great interest to both cases. They allowed the god of chaos to go first. Set wove together a tale of deception, claiming that the throne was rightfully his after the death of Osiris. However, Horus was not to be discouraged. When it was his turn to speak to the gods, he claimed that the throne was his right after his father was murdered.

Set, however, was not convinced. Because Horus had the head of a hawk, he pointed out to the trifecta that Horus would not be a good leader to Egypt. He claimed that since ravens were considered bad luck and Horus was closely affiliated with them due to his aviary nature, Horus would bring about the downfall of the Egyptian way of life.

While Thoth and Shu believed that Horus should be given the throne, Ra remained unconvinced. Because he was the oldest god and his opinion was not voiced first, he cast his vote on Set. He claimed that Set was the stronger of the two, and his strength would forever carry the weight of responsibility. In addition, Set also had more experience as a ruler than Horus.

The vote, however, required that all three gods have the same opinion. When the gods could not agree on a vote, they introduced the concept of a small series of trials to commence. Whoever won the most trials would be declared the rightful king to the throne.

The First Trial: Hippopotami

Set thought of a competition only he could win and decided on the first trial. The first trial was simple enough: the two gods would have to transform into hippopotami and sink to the bottom of the Nile. Whoever could hold their breath the longest would win. Both gods transformed into hippopotami and sank to the bottom of the Nile.

Isis doubted her son's capabilities. She knew that Horus needed to win this trial to cement his position as the rightful heir to the throne. She crafted a weapon to wound Set but ended up hitting Horus instead. Realizing her mistake, she aimed for Set and wounded him as well. Both gods emerged from the depths simultaneously, which voided the results.

In his anger, Horus decapitated his mother for interfering. The trifecta of gods did not approve of this choice and refused to overlook this behavior. The result deemed Set as the winner of the trial. Enraged, Horus stormed off and awaited the next trial.

After the trial, the kind god of wisdom Thoth revived Isis, granting her another chance at life.

The Second Trial: Fight Over Dominance

As a word of warning, this next trial is rather graphic, and not one that everyone would be comfortable reading.

During the night, Set attempted to sodomize Horus to assert his dominance over the young god. Horus, however, would not allow this humiliation to happen. He fooled Set into believing he was successful in his attempt, but Horus instead had collected Set's semen in his hands. Horus sought advice from his mother, Isis, who when seeing the semen in her son's hands chopped them off and threw them into the Nile. In his revenge, Horus put his own semen on some lettuce. Before the trial, Horus gave Set a gift of this lettuce, which was his favorite food. He ate the lettuce, unknowing of what Horus had done to it.

Set had arranged for the tribune of gods to observe the domination over Horus by claiming his witnesses were inside the body of the young god. However, this was not the case. When Set called out to his witnesses, all was silent. Then, Horus called upon his own seed as witnesses, and since they were inside the body of Set, it was agreed that Horus had won the trial.

The Third Trial: Boat Racing

Both Set and Horus had their groups of followers and believers. However, the trio of gods could not make a fair assessment and so they decided on one last trial: a boat race. The trial was simple and required boats to be carved out of stone and raced. Whoever crossed the finish line first would be considered the rightful ruler of Egypt.

The competing gods quickly got to work on their boats. Set crafted a beautiful boat made of stone. He was proud of the boat he had carved and believed that he could win the race. Horus crafted his boat out of wood instead of stone and then plastered it with a lighter stone to give it the appearance of stone.

The race began, and Horus was in the lead due to the boat's buoyancy. Set's boat, however, moved slowly and eventually sank into the Nile. Set was mocked and ridiculed for his easy defeat. Horus finished the race but not before the god of chaos morphed into a hippopotamus and revealed the deception inside Horus's boat. The gods conceded that Horus was disqualified for cheating while Set was disqualified for unsportsmanlike conduct. As a result, the final trial commenced.

The Final Trial: Letters to Osiris

The gods still could not come to a unanimous vote, so they believed the original ruler should have a say in the new ruler of Egypt. Each god was tasked with writing a letter to the god of the Underworld, justifying their claims to the throne.

Osiris read each letter and gave his final verdict. He ruled in favor of his son because he believed that no one had the right to rule over Egypt after murdering the previous king. The other deities agreed with this ruling, and Set was sentenced to exile in the desert. Henceforth, he was then known as the god of the desert and storms.

Other Retellings

Some versions of the myth had different endings to numerous battles between Horus and Set. For example, some versions claimed that Set was not sentenced to exile, but instead was killed by Horus. While this was a satisfying end to the reign of terror that Set had brought upon the Egyptians, it was not the only version of this story.

Other versions of the myth portrayed Horus as a kind and forgiving god, and he and Set had agreed to split the land into two parts, each representing their rule. Horus gained the realm of Upper Egypt with the most valuable cities in the land, while Set was allowed to rule over Lower Egypt, which was known for its desert.

The Aftermath

The removal of Set allowed the kingdom to restore balance and order to the Egyptians. This resulted in peace that followed for many years under the rule of Horus. As Horus rebuilt Egypt from the havoc that Set's reign had produced, he was able to reinstate Isis as the reigning queen and his aunt Nephthys as his counselor. His presence in the kingdom ushered in a new era of peace.

Conclusion

This myth was packed with action, betrayal, humiliation, and indecisive gods who, in the end, made the right decision. The many battles between Horus and Set cemented their place in history as one of the most convoluted trials to determine a ruler. Because Horus was successful and deemed the indisputable heir to the throne, the divine right to rule overshadowed any previous doubts. Due to the next generations of kings and pharaohs believing they were descended from the gods themselves, the future kings of Egypt celebrated Horus and considered themselves to be Horus reincarnated. While this myth was considered to be one of the greatest and most important myths, it also warned of the repercussions of committing a deadly sin. Murder and rape, especially of a young king, were then punishable by dire means.

The next chapter will be a myth that is a little lighter in mood and context. This next story weaves a tale about love and the importance of patience. The story itself may feel familiar, so keep reading to find out why.

Chapter 6: The Girl with the

Rose-Red Slippers

"The Girl with the Rose-Red Slippers" was a tale about fated lovers and romance. This myth revolved around a young Greek woman by the name of Rhodopis who was enslaved in an Egyptian city. She lost a precious item of hers and feared it would never return, but then, a surprise visitor appeared at her door and the two eventually married. If this story seems a little too familiar, the reason is that this myth was the first written rendition of the common fairytale "Cinderella."

The ancient Egyptians believed all aspects of life were important, and the stories of love and romance resonate with many people. The ancient Egyptians may have had morbid tendencies in their storytelling, but one of their romance stories is still prominent in popular culture today.

The Enslaved Life of Rhodopis

According to the myth, the main protagonist in this story, a beautiful Greek woman by the name of Rhodopis, was a young, shy, and quiet woman. For most of her young life, she was enslaved and kept by rich men. She was often tasked with cooking, cleaning, and taking care of the house, similar to the tasks of the other slaves on the island where she was kept. Her story was quite tragic in the beginning, but in time, she was able to gain the heart of an entire empire.

Kidnapped by Pirates and Sold into Slavery

Rhodopis never knew her parents. She had been kidnapped by pirates when she was very young. The pirates sold her to a slaver in Greece who profited from her kidnapping and eventual enslavement. Because she was so small, she was nursed and taken care of by the other slaves. The man who bought her lived on the island of Samos where he had an abundance of slaves.

The young woman was quiet and shy but also very kind. She had many close friendships with the other slaves, especially Aesop. Aesop was considered to be an ugly, old, but kind man who always spun together tales and fantasies of wildlife and magic. His stories entranced her. In those moments, her woes washed away.

As a child, Rhodopis dreamt of a land where she could be free from her enslavement. When she fully matured into a young, beautiful woman, her slaver decided that he could profit off of her beauty. She was forced to leave her previous life behind and become another man's property in Egypt.

The slave boat made port at the Egyptian city of Naucratis a short time later. Disoriented, she was then thrown into a cage to be put on display on the streets of the city. The streets were also home to many Greeks as a way for the pharaoh to open up trade. The pharaoh at the time was known as Amasis, and he considered this port city to be one of the crucial ports for trading, which also included the slave trade. He was also in fear and wanted to bolster his allies to help them ward off the Persian Empire.

The city was almost entirely made up of Greek culture, but there were still many Egyptians who lived there. In the middle of Naucratis, the slave trade boomed.

Looking around the city, it seemed that all was doomed for the young Rhodopis. As the other slaves were auctioned off, she feared a fate worse than death. However, lurking in the crowd, an old Greek man had taken notice of her beauty. As the bidding began, the old man raised the bid and bought her.

Charaxos

As the old man claimed his prize, he said his name was Charaxos. He was a rich merchant who had retired to the city after a lifetime of trading with Egypt. Charaxos was in awe of her beauty, as was everyone else, and chauffeured his prize home. Instead of remaining quiet, she instead told him the chronicles of her life so far. The tale moved Charaxos deeply, and he even pitied the poor young woman. He wanted to help her as much as he could, and as time passed, he took on the role of a father.

The New Life of Luxury

Charaxos was immediately taken aback when he gazed upon the pale-skinned beauty with dark flowing hair and rosy cheeks. She was like a newfound daughter to him, and he gave her everything she desired. Even though Charaxos never had children, he was drawn to her and wanted to protect her. Over time, the two grew closer. They both were happy. The gifts he gave her included a house with a garden in the courtyard located in the middle of the home, slaves to wait on her, and numerous outfits and jewelry.

The Rose-Red Slippers

One of the gifts she cherished the most was a gorgeous outfit complete with a pair of rose-colored shoes and a belt adorned with jewels. She often wore this outfit out to the various parties and social gatherings she was now privy to. In addition to this outfit, she spent most of her time outside in the garden. The garden itself held a beautifully ornate marble bathtub in the middle of it, where she would bathe and watch the nature.

Scene of the Crime

It was a typical day in the household. Rhodopis often took baths in the middle of the day during the summer to help cool her off. She stripped in the courtyard as the slave women got the bath ready for her. She rested her slippers and girdle on the table on the far side of the courtyard. Once the bath was drawn, the slave women then guarded her most cherished possessions.

She lay in the bath, relishing the cool water against her skin. She positioned herself to watch the nature as she usually did, when suddenly an eagle swooped down and gripped one of the shoes in its talons. The slave women quickly dispersed, running away out of fear and shock. Rhodopis, too, was shocked. She stood up in her bath as the eagle claimed its prize, but as quickly as it came, it left. A gasp of horror escaped from the young Rhodopis. She watched the eagle as it flew away in the direction of the Nile to an unknown destination. Distraught, she removed herself from the bath and wept in her room.

Arrival of Fate

The eagle flew to Memphis where the pharaoh Amasis sat in his grand courtyard, listening to his constituents. He heeded their problems with an open heart and made decisions based on how to best protect and provide for his people. The task could be daunting, but he only wanted health, happiness, and harmony for the Egyptians.

The same eagle landed in front of the king, blocking his vision of one of the peasants in front of him. The eagle dropped the shoe in front of him and stared at him for a few brief moments before ultimately leaving to soar through the skies.

Amasis clutched the shoe in front of him. Believing this to be a sign from Horus, the god of pharaohs, he closely examined the contents of the shoe. It was well-made with expensive material and with intricate detail, including the small and delicate jewels lining the outside; he knew that the owner of the shoe would be just as exquisite.

He proclaimed his will to find the owner of the shoe, return it to her, and bring her back to Memphis as his bride. Sending his messengers to all the cities in Egypt, he stayed in Memphis until his future bride was discovered.

A New Life of Luxury

After several months, the pharaoh felt impatient with the lack of news from his messengers. They had scoured far and wide for an owner with the same shoe, but to no avail. Some families tried to counterfeit the shoe, but each claim proved to be false. Finally, there was a rumor that the true owner of the slipper was a young Greek woman who lived with one of the wealthiest men in Naucratis. One of the messengers reported the rumor to the Amasis. Trusting his advisors, he set sail toward the great city and vowed to not return to Memphis until he found the rightful owner of the shoe.

The Lovers Finally Unite

Amasis and some of his messengers docked at the port into Naucratis. Once they were in the city, he asked several of the passersby on the street where he could find the woman with the rose-red shoe. Some of them were new to the city, but there was a slave woman who knew where the young Greek woman lived. She then gave directions to Amasis and his men. The slave woman had said the young woman was once a slave like herself, but then a man with a kind soul bought her and treated her like a long-lost daughter. Amasis knew that this woman was the correct owner, and relieved, he went to the home of Rhodopis.

Rhodopis was home in the garden when she heard a knock at her door. Not expecting anyone, she cautiously opened the door and was greatly surprised to see the Pharaoh on her doorstep.

Amasis was blown away by her beauty. He then showed her the shoe that was stolen several months beforehand. She cried out in relief that her precious slipper had finally returned to her. When she extended her foot, Amasis slipped the shoe on her delicate foot and discovered that it was truly hers. Rhodopis then asked her slaves to retrieve the shoe's twin so the pair could be reunited.

An Unusual Marriage Proposal

After it was confirmed that Rhodopis was the woman he had searched for, he then decreed that she needed to return to Memphis with him to be his queen. It was an offer she could not refuse. Not only was the word of pharaoh law, but she also was very attracted to him. She quickly packed her belongings with the help of her slaves and said her farewells to Charaxos, who had taken care of her well. Charaxos was hesitant to see her leave, but he knew that she would be provided for.

When the two returned to Memphis, Amasis then married Rhodopis. It was said that the couple then enjoyed a life of harmony, health, and luxury, even until their deaths. According to legend, they died on the same day to journey through the afterlife together.

The Other Version

In other variations of this myth, it was more of a true rags-to-riches story that more closely mirrors the actual story of

Cinderella. In this version, Rhodopis was still enslaved, but not to a kind and gentle old man. Instead, she was often forced to hide her slippers from the other slaves who would be tempted to steal them. For her, the shoes were the only part of her previous life that she remembered. She could not remember what connected them to her and her family because she was taken away from them at a very young age.

She lived and worked in a large house on one of the banks of the Nile River, which was heavily populated with slaves. The male slaves and the men who visited the home constantly gawked at her beauty. The other slave women grew jealous of the attention she garnered from the men, believing that she also had an air of arrogance. Young Rhodopis was quiet and shy, scarcely reacting to the advances the men would make.

The slaves knew that Rhodopis held onto a priceless treasure: rose-red shoes and delicate jewels. The jealous women tried to locate the treasure, but Rhodopis hid them too well.

The Secret Hiding Spot

After a long day's work, she often removed the slippers from their hiding place and watched the jewels catch the light of both the sun and moon. She was fascinated by the numerous colors that shone from the jewels. When she was satisfied and her mood lifted, she placed them back in her hiding spot until the next time she needed to feel better.

One night, she could not manage to fall asleep. The night was quiet, and she decided to gaze at the jewels on her shoes in the moonlight. Rhodopis then went to her designated hiding spot where she admired the light shimmering on the jewels. The lighting entranced her, and her troubles were gone for a few short moments. As she put the shoes back, an eagle descended from the night sky and stole one of her shoes. Once she realized the shoe was lost forever, she went back to her cot and wept until she fell asleep.

The (Almost) Same Resolution

The main plot of the story remained the same in this version, but there were some differences. One of the advisors of Amasis found out her location and had her try on the shoe within four days. Pleased with her looks, the advisor knew the king would be grateful that such a woman existed. The Pharaoh was immediately smitten with her upon seeing her for the first time, and they married soon after.

When the advisor arrived at the home, one of the other slave women answered. He inquired about the slave woman who had lost an intriguing red colored shoe with jewels. In his mind, this woman would have no way of owning the shoe's twin; if it was a false claim, she would be punished.

Believing that the Pharaoh was at the home to punish Rhodopis for keeping such a treasured heirloom, she escorted the advisor, who then demanded proof that she was indeed the owner of the shoe. Rhodopis then showed the advisor where she had hidden the other shoe. Taken aback that the slave woman was indeed telling the truth, he ordered her to follow him to Memphis to become the queen of Egypt.

The family whom she served was upset about one of their slaves being taken away, but the advisor bestowed on them a bracelet made of pure gold as payment for her. She was then escorted back to Memphis where she married the Pharaoh and had a life of happiness with him.

Conclusion

Not all of the myths from the Egyptian pantheon consisted of death and darkness. While the ancient Egyptians were fascinated by death, it did not completely rule over their lives. They also believed that love was a powerful force by itself. According to the myth, love was a gift that was granted and blessed by the gods. However, this myth withstood the test of time. Not only has this same story been told over many generations with many variations, but the belief of a happily ever after was a breath of fresh air in the many myths revolving around violence. However, in the next chapter, violence is once again at the heart of the myth.

Chapter 7: The Eye of Horus

The Eye of Horus is a widely-known symbol for healing, protection, and all-seeing. The myth recounted a tale that the loss of his eye was the fault of Set in their many battles and trials. It's not surprising that the loss of his eye was caused by Set, given their record of 80 years of conflict. The myth has several variations, including the graphic details of the story or the lack thereof. There are several conflicting narrations, and in this chapter, two of the versions will be discussed. Each myth differs from the others in its many details, from which deity reconstructed the eye to the location of its loss.

Battle Over the Kingdom

Chapter 5 chronicled the tale of Horus and Set and their battle for power. Set, in some myths, was portrayed as a liar and the epitome of evil and jealousy. While the personality of Set has already been established, he paved the way for one of the most widely-recognized symbols of all time.

The Loss of the Eye During Battle

Set and Horus often engaged in a battle for dominance and the right to rule over Egypt. In one version of the myth, the loss of the eye was the result of Set cheating and attempting to assert his claim to the throne. The two engaged in a sparring match. It was said that the two were evenly matched, but Set wanted to ensure that he would win the claim to the throne.

At one point, Set was almost able to fully overpower Horus in an armed duel. In one swift movement, Set ripped out his opponent's left eye. Horus doubled over in pain. Set gloated at his easy victory. However, Horus was not to be made a fool. When Set was distracted, Horus hit Set in the groin, rupturing his testicles. According to the tribunal, the gods were yet again at a stalemate.

Thoth was able to fully restore the eye, and Set's testicles made a full recovery without even a scar. According to the myth, the left eye was connected to the moon and its waning and waxing cycles. Because the eye was fully restored by Thoth, it was then perceived as restoring order from chaos.

Picking Up the Pieces

In another myth, Horus had his eye removed by none other than Set as he was sleeping. After one of the battles where Horus was defeated, he situated himself in a remote location and eventually fell asleep. Under the cover of darkness, Set crept up to the sleeping Horus and ripped out his eye. Horus awoke with a start and screamed in pain. He could not see Set, but he knew that the god of chaos was behind the attack.

Victorious, he ripped the eye into six pieces and scattered them in the Nile, not dissimilar to how he treated the body of Osiris so many years prior. The pieces floated down the Nile and he believed that he would not be defeated during their next battle.

Horus recruited help from Hathor, the goddess of love. They scoured the Nile for all the pieces of the eye, but could only find five of the six. Horus and Hathor then recruited Thoth to assemble the broken pieces. Thoth took the pieces in his hands and added a magical element so that Horus was able to see the invisible as well as what was to come.

Conclusion

The Eye of Horus was a huge symbol within ancient Egyptian culture. Due to its magical power and the symbolic meaning of protection, the left eye of Horus was ingrained in ancient Egyptian culture. It was crafted onto amulets to protect their wearer and was even painted on boats for protection against the harms of the sea. The Eye of Horus, with its many mystical powers, including its all-seeing power, had cemented its impact on Egyptian civilization and is still abundantly used to this day. Another eye that is often conflated with the Eye of Horus will be covered in the next chapter in a myth about destruction and the potential end of humanity.

Chapter 8: The Eye of Ra

The Eye of Ra, which was Ra's right eye, should not be confused with the Eye of Horus despite some texts swapping the symbols around. The Eye of Ra was another symbol of power, protection, and the sun, as opposed to the Eye of Horus representing the moon. However, its many powers tended to overlap with the Eye of Horus, which led to confusion between them. It was forever symbolized as a disk representing the sun and a pair of uraeus cobras that encircled the disk. One myth of Ra stood out from the rest, highlighting its destructive power.

The Near Destruction of Mankind

The Eye of Ra was a symbol of not only the power of pharaohs but also illustrated the destructive power of the sun. In some versions of the myth, the Eye of Ra also represented the goddesses who were related to Ra such as Hathor, Nut, and others. Hathor, however, was the goddess who played a major role in this myth. The eye was used as a weapon against humanity after Ra had been disappointed by the people he created, thus signifying the end of his creation.

Set's Work Was Finished

After the death of Osiris, Set welcomed a new era of men complete with negative traits such as war, famine, murder, and even greed. The rise of Set had rendered all previous laws useless, and the world was thrown into a storm of chaos. After Horus regained the throne, there was much work to be redone, and the gods and people started to rebuild the kingdom.

However, Set's work had already been done. While the physical aspects of the land were rebuilt, humanity as a whole became deeply troubled. The once pure-hearted Egyptians now had darkness within them that could not be undone. They essentially were shells of what they used to be, and hiding within them were the attributes related to corruption and brutality. There was no return to the light after the darkness crept into the hearts of men.

The Disappointment of the Sun God

According to the myth, the sun god Ra had come back to earth after he was finished with the creation of the universe. He was excited to see how far the civilization had expanded, and what kind of advancements they had made in his absence. Proud of his achievements and his creation he returned to the earth. However, when he returned, the realm was not the same as he had left it. In an instant, he detected the festering corruption of his creation.

The sun god was immensely disappointed at his creation. Not only were they far off from the evolution he had predicted but there was still evidence of Set's corruptive influence. Some of the buildings were still in disrepair, there was the distinct odor of dried blood that had been spilled, and the eyes of the people looked haunted and scared instead of happy and content.

Instead of empathizing with his creation, Ra instead grew angry. At the time, he had not realized the extent of Set's power and therefore was angry at the people for devolving into nothing better than savages. As a result, he ordered a genocide of his people.

The Eye of Ra

To fully punish the people, Ra called upon Hathor. Using the power of his eye, he then transformed the gentle loving goddess into a harbinger of death called Sekhmet. Sekhmet was a goddess of war with a lioness's head on the body of a woman. Ra ordered her to kill any human that stood in her way.

Sekhmet massacred many of the people of Egypt without remorse, enjoying the fulfillment of her duty. The more blood she spilled, the more she craved.

Ra at first watched with pleasure as Sekhmet slaughtered the humans in her path. However, her bloodthirsty rage had gone on for long enough. The goddess showed no signs of stopping, and the murderous glint in her eye grew brighter with each kill. Ra, then overcome with guilt and worry over completely ending his creation, proceeded to call her off. She did not heed his warning, and the sun god was forced to subdue the goddess.

Subduing Sekhmet

Subduing her would not be an easy task. Ra then crafted an idea consisting of beer and red dye to lull her to sleep. Once beer and pomegranates were collected, the plan was set in motion. Over 7000 gallons of beer and pomegranate juice in total were gathered and he mixed the juice in with the beer to give it the crimson color she sought, which was then littered around the city. Sekhmet then drank the alcoholic mixture.

Once she had her fill, Sekhmet then fell into a deep slumber due to the high content of alcohol. According to legend, she slept for three days straight and woke up feeling refreshed. After she had risen, Ra removed his eye from Sekhmet and she returned to the goddess Hathor. Even though the majority of humanity had been devoured, they were able to rebuild. Ra vowed to never use such drastic measures against his creation again.

Conclusion

The myth of Ra and his eye is not as common as the famous symbol of the Eye of Horus. However, the myth illustrated the destructive power of his eye, which was then used as a symbol of protection. This symbol of protection and its destructive power has cemented its place in history.

The ancient Egyptian civilization was at one point a world power, and it's easy to see why. With their resources and power over the people, the Egyptians represented a time in human history when myths and legends were at the heart of the belief system of its people. This was reflected in everything from funerary rites to the many dynasties believing in the divine right to rule. The civilization, together with its many deities in the pantheon and its myths and legends, is one of the most interesting civilizations that still inspires awe and wonder. Even though there are still many mysteries revolving around ancient Egypt, its mythology provides fascinating lessons and adventure.

References

Bhandari, S. (2022, September 10). *How Long Did The Egyptian Empire Last(And Why)?*. Exactly How Long. https://exactlyhowlong.com/how-long-did-the-egyptian-empire-lastand-why/

Castillo, J. A. H. (2022, May 24). *Egyptian Mythology Creatures and Monsters*. Study.Com. https://study.com/learn/lesson/egyptian-mythological-creatures-list-folklore-symbolism.html

The Conflict between Horus and Seth over the Throne of Ancient Egypt. (2022a, April 19). World History Edu. https://www.worldhistoryedu.com/the-conflict-between-horus-and-seth-over-the-throne-of-ancient-egypt/

Daily Life in Ancient Egypt. (n.d.). Ancient Egypt Online. Retrieved November 4, 2022, from https://www.ancient-egypt-online.com/daily-life-in-ancient-egypt.html

Donn, L. (n.d.). *An Ancient Egyptian Cinderella Story: The Red Slippers*. Mr. Donn's Site for Kids and Teachers. Retrieved November 8, 2022, from https://egypt.mrdonn.org/redslippers.html

The Editors of Encyclopaedia Britannica. (n.d.). *11 Egyptian Gods and Goddesses*. Britannica. Retrieved November 6, 2022, from https://www.britannica.com/list/11-egyptian-gods-and-goddesses

The Editors of Encyclopaedia Britannica. (2022, October 26). *Eye of Horus*. Britannica. Retrieved November 6, 2022, from https://www.britannica.com/topic/Eye-of-Horus

EGYPTIAN GOD. (2021, January 21). Egyptian History. https://egyptian-history.com/blogs/egyptian-gods/egyptian-gods

EYE OF HORUS. (2020a, December 5). Egyptian History. https://egyptian-history.com/blogs/egyptian-symbols/eye-of-horus

The Eye of Ra. (n.d.). Ancient Egypt Online. Retrieved November 9, 2022, from https://www.ancient-egypt-online.com/eye-of-ra.html

EYE OF RA. (2020, December 12). Egyptian History. https://egyptian-history.com/blogs/egyptian-symbols/eye-of-re

Gill, N. S. (2019, March 28). *Egyptian Creation Myths: The Main Cosmologies of Ancient Egypt*. Learn Religions. https://www.learnreligions.com/egyptian-creation-myths-4590184

The Girl with the Rose Red Slippers. (2019, December 11). Ancient Egypt: *The Mythology*. http://www.egyptianmyths.net/mythslippers.htm

Horus: Birth Story, Family, Eye of Horus, Powers, & Symbols. (2020, January 9). World History Edu. https://www.worldhistoryedu.com/horus-the-ancient-egyptian-god-of-the-sky/

Lary, M. H. (2022, November 4). *Ptah: Egypt's God of Crafts and Creation*. History Cooperative. https://historycooperative.org/ptah/

Mandal, D. (2022, August 10). *12 Fascinating Ancient Egyptian Mythological Creatures*. Realm of History. https://www.realmofhistory.com/2022/08/10/egyptian -mythological-creatures/

Mark, J. J. (2013, January 17). *Ancient Egyptian Mythology*. World History Encyclopedia. https://www.worldhistory.org/Egyptian_Mythology/

Mark, J. J. (2016a, September 21). *Daily Life in Ancient Egypt*. World History Encyclopedia. https://www.worldhistory.org/article/933/daily-life-in-ancient-egypt/

Mark, J. J. (2016b, April 14). *Egyptian Gods—The Complete List*. World History Encyclopedia. https://www.worldhistory.org/article/885/egyptian-gods---the-complete-list/

Mark, J. J. (2017, March 17). *Festivals in Ancient Egypt*. World History Encyclopedia. https://www.worldhistory.org/article/1032/festivals-in-ancient-egypt/

The Myth of Osiris and Isis. (2022b, April 19). World History Edu. https://www.worldhistoryedu.com/the-myth-of-osiris-and-isis/

Professor Geller. (2016a, December 8). *Eye of Horus*. Mythology.Net. https://mythology.net/egyptian/egyptian-concepts/eye-of-horus/

Professor Geller. (2016b, October 11). *Ptah*. Mythology.Net. https://mythology.net/egyptian/egyptian-gods/ptah/

SET AND HORUS. (2021, January 10). Egyptian History. https://egyptian-history.com/blogs/egyptian-gods/set-vs-horus

Strauss, B. (2019, July 3). *Monsters and Mythical Creatures of Ancient Egypt.* ThoughtCo. https://www.thoughtco.com/egyptian-monsters-4145424

Way of Life in Ancient Egypt. (n.d.). South African History Online. Retrieved November 8, 2022, from https://www.sahistory.org.za/article/way-life-ancient-egypt

What Were the Ancient Egyptian Creation Myths. (n.d.). DailyHistory.org. Retrieved November 8, 2022, from https://dailyhistory.org/What_Were_the_Ancient_Egyptian_Creation_Myths

Webber, F. (2020, March 4). *List of the Top 15 Best Egyptian Myths You Should Know About.* Dreams & Myths. https://dreamsandmythology.com/best-egyptian-myths/

Wegner, J. H. (2021, July 13). *Ancient Egyptian Creation Myths: From Watery Chaos to Cosmic Egg.* Glencairn Museum News. https://www.glencairnmuseum.org/newsletter/2021/7/13/ancient-egyptian-creation-myths-from-watery-chaos-to-cosmic-egg

www.ingramcontent.com/pod-product-compliance
Lightning Source LLC
Chambersburg PA
CBHW070938120626
46546CB00004B/1469